Our Emotions and Behaviour

But Why Can't I?

Written by Sue Graves

Illustrated by

Desideria Guicciardini

W

FRANKLIN WATTS

LONDON • SYDNEY

Jenny came to look after George and his sister, Rosie. Mum told them the rules.

They had to go to bed at 7 o'clock. They had to listen to Jenny. They had to keep to the **rules.**

But George said rules **were silly!**

Jenny took them to the park.
They had to cross a road.

Jenny said there were **rules** for crossing roads.
They had to **stop, look** and **listen.**

But George didn't **stop, look** or **listen.**
He nearly ran into **the road!**

Jenny said **rules** can keep people safe!

Later on, Jenny got out a **game**.
She told them the **rules**.
They had to take turns to throw the dice.

But George didn't listen.
He didn't take turns.
No one could **play.**

So Jenny had to put the **game** away.

She said rules make *playing* games *fair!*

Then Jenny said it was **7 o'clock**.
It was time for bed.
But George didn't want to go to bed.
He wanted to stay up **late**.

"But why can't I?" he moaned.
Jenny said he needed his sleep.
She said people need sleep to keep
fit and **well**.

But George didn't listen.
He stayed up **late**. He got
tired and **grumpy**.

Then Jenny told him that she had to keep **rules**, too.

She told him she worked in a shop.
The shop had lots of customers.
It was a great place to work.

But she had to keep to the **rules.**
She had to look smart for work.

She had to get to work **on time**, too.

But one day Jenny was **late** for work. The customers could not get into the shop. Everyone was **cross.**

Jenny nearly lost her job.
She was **never late again!**

George was really tired now.
He yawned and **yawned.**

George got under the blanket.
He said rules weren't silly at all!

Can you tell the story of Emma dropping her drink can on the path?

How do you think the boy who tripped over felt?

Why do you think Emma should use the bin?

A note about sharing this book

The *Our Emotions and Behaviour* series has been developed to provide a starting point for further discussion on children's feelings and behaviour, both in relation to themselves and to other people.

But Why Can't I?
This story explores in a reassuring way why we have rules and how rules can make everyone's lives easier and safer.

The book aims to encourage children to have a developing awareness of behavioural expectations in different settings. It also invites children to begin to consider the consequences of their words and actions for themselves and others.

Storyboard puzzle
The wordless storyboard on pages 26 and 27 provides an opportunity for speaking and listening. Children are encouraged to tell the story illustrated in the panels: Emma drops her drink can on the path rather than using the bin. A boy skates up and trips over the can. He is cross and Emma feels bad. She learns that using the bin might be a good rule after all.

How to use the book
The book is designed for adults to share with either an individual child, or a group of children, and as a starting point for discussion.

The book also provides visual support and repeated words and phrases to build confidence in children who are starting to read on their own.

Before reading the story
Choose a time to read when you and the children are relaxed and have time to share the story.

Spend time looking at the illustrations and talk about what the book may be about before reading it together.

After reading, talk about the book with the children:

- What was it about? Have the children ever been looked after by a babysitter? Did Mum or Dad lay down some rules? What were they? Did the children stick to the rules? If not, what were the consequences?

  Encourage the children to talk about their experiences.

- Extend this discussion by talking about other rules they know. Examples might be rules at home, rules in school and rules when visiting other people's homes. Invite the children to talk about these rules and identify why they are important.

- Now talk about rules that apply to adults. Some examples might be parking restrictions, road rules, etc. Why do they think these rules are important? Conversely, can they think of any rules that they consider silly? Discuss the merits or otherwise of these rules.

- Take the opportunity to talk about rules that the children would like to see imposed to make their own lives easier. Examples might be stopping parents from parking too close to the school gates when dropping off and collecting their children.

- Look at the storyboard puzzle. Can the children talk about Emma dropping her drink can on the path? Can they discuss why it would have been better for Emma to use the bin?

Can they think of other rules that help to keep us safe in the park?

Choose two settings, for example, at school, in the playground, in the supermarket, at the swimming pool.

Make a list of rules for each setting and draw picture signs to decorate your rules lists. Compare the two lists. Are some rules the same? Are there any differences? Why?

Franklin Watts
This edition published in Great Britain in 2014 by the Watts Publishing Group

Copyrigh text © Franklin Watts 2013
Copyright illustrations © Desideria Guicciardini 2013

The rights of Sue Graves to be identified as the author
and Desideria Guicciardini as the illustrator of this Work have
been asserted in accordance with the Copyright, Designs
and Patents Act, 1988.

A CIP catalogue record for this book is available
from the British Library.

ISBN 978 1 4451 2990 7

Editor: Jackie Hamley
Designer: Peter Scoulding

Printed in China

Franklin Watts
An imprint of
Hachette Children's Group
Part of The Watts Publishing Group
Carmelite House
50 Victoria Embankment
London EC4Y 0DZ

An Hachette UK Company
www.hachette.co.uk

www.franklinwatts.co.uk

MIX
Paper from
responsible sources
FSC® C104740
FSC
www.fsc.org